Holly . Browning.

C000183203

THE CONCISE HISTORY OF
WWII

THE CONCISE HISTORY OF
WWII

First published in the UK in 2013

© Demand Media Limited 2013

www.demand-media.co.uk

Printed and bound in China

ISBN 978-1-909217-36-2

Contents

Introduction

By 1938 war in Europe seemed inevitable. It had only been twenty years since the war to end all wars, and the horrors of conflict were still fresh in the mind, but that didn't stop all sides re-arming and preparing for yet more bloodshed. Germany may have been defeated in 1918 but it remained the largest and most powerful nation-state on the continent.

Many believed that the settlement at the end of World War One was neither clean nor decisive. The treaty signed at Versailles didn't make much of an allowance for peace as it punished Germany by confiscating territory and forcing the people to pay reparations to help rebuild France and reduce the Allied debt to America. The German army was to be almost completely demilitarised, deprived of its modern weapons and slashed to a fraction of its former size. So instead of negating Germany as a threat, the settlement led to deep-seated anger and resentment among its people. These feelings were only heightened when the country's economy spiralled out of control in the early 1920s. The downturn left millions penniless and contributed to more bitterness in what was the country's darkest hour.

The people believed that they hadn't been beaten in battle and had actually been betrayed on the Western Front by incompetent leaders and at home by

Above: *The League of Nations building in Geneva*

cowardly and weak politicians. They needed someone to turn to who would relieve them from their suffering and who would avenge the humiliation heaped on them by the West.

The Americans, British and French drew up proposals for a League of Nations that would resolve international disputes by diplomatic rather than military means. The old and worryingly powerful Austro-Hungarian Empire was dissolved into smaller, weaker states

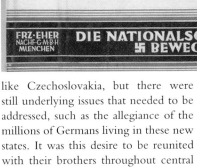

like Czechoslovakia, but there were still underlying issues that needed to be addressed, such as the allegiance of the millions of Germans living in these new states. It was this desire to be reunited with their brothers throughout central Europe that was the time-bomb waiting to explode.

President Woodrow Wilson was overruled by congress on his return to the US and America was forced to withdraw from the League of Nations.

Without its most powerful member, the league was bereft of the strength it would need should territorial disputes arise.

Germany's fledgling Weimar Republic was immediately threatened when right-wing nationalists clashed with revolutionary communists. Tension escalated when ordinary people's savings were wiped out during the hyperinflationary years and economic turmoil. The time was right for a skilled orator – who worked receptive audiences by preaching extreme right-wing views – to begin his ascent to power.

Adolf Hitler had been born in Austria but he'd fought for Germany with distinction in the First World War. After the conflict he returned to Munich and was soon recruiting followers to the once-marginalised National Socialist Party. In October 1923 Hitler believed he had enough support to overthrow

the republic but he was stabbed in the back by supposedly loyal followers and the coup failed. He was imprisoned for nine months, during which time he wrote *Mein Kampf* (*My Struggle*), which blamed Germany's weak economy on the Jews and claimed the way to solve the country's problems was to seize territory in Eastern Europe.

When he was released he realised he could only assume power via legitimate democratic means so he used his oratorical skills to recruit more people to the cause. But when the Weimar Republic survived the economic downturn in the early 1920s and brought five years of prosperity, support for the extremists dwindled. It seemed the national socialists would be consigned to history.

In 1929, however, Hitler was thrown a lifeline when the US stock market crashed. This Great Depression swept across the world and unemployment

reached six million in Germany by the end of the decade. Hitler used the unrest in the country to recruit millions of young people to the Nazi movement and he soon offered a viable political alternative.

In the 1932 elections, Hitler's Nazis became the dominant force in Germany's parliament but he refused to form a coalition. To avoid political as well as economic turmoil, in January 1933 President Hindenburg proclaimed Hitler Germany's chancellor, the head of its government. A month later the Reichstag burned down so Hitler was given emergency powers and he immediately banned all other political parties. He may have risen to power democratically but he then abolished the freedoms by which he'd been elected. When Hindenburg died the following year, Hitler declared himself Führer, absolute leader of all Germany.

Hitler initially concentrated on rebuilding German confidence and lowering its runaway unemployment. He put millions back to work building the autobahn system but he was also secretly ignoring the constraints of the Treaty of Versailles by beginning a huge program of re-armament. For

two years the country stockpiled arms and machinery until, in 1935, Hitler blatantly flouted the conditions imposed by the West when he unveiled his new air force, the Luftwaffe. Later that year the French-occupied Saarland voted to return to German rule, and in 1936 Germany reoccupied the demilitarised Rhineland. Britain and France didn't object because they knew the territories and population were rightfully German.

Hitler wasn't alone with his expansionist aspirations: in the Far East, Japan's military pretensions manifested itself in the invasion of China in 1937. Japan was a global power and had been a member of the League of Nations, but the country was a confusing blend of democracy, outdated but popular feudal traditions, and an all-powerful emperor

Above: *Italian artillery on the Abyssinian border in 1936*

Far Left: *Chiang Kai-shek commanded Allied forces in China from 1942 to 1945*

THE CONCISE HISTORY OF **WWII**

who was viewed as a living god. Its population was exploding and it needed natural resources to feed and house them. They already had troops in Manchuria and could also look to expand into the British colonies like Burma, Malaya and Hong Kong; the French outpost of Indochina; and the Dutch East Indies. The US held various small territories in the Pacific but they had downsized their navy after the Great War and were not strong enough to counter any Japanese aggression. With the US suffering in the depression, Japan made its first move into the mainland in 1931 but it was another six years before they struck at the heart of China. With Mao Tsetung and Chiang Kai-shek battling one another for political control, China was in turmoil and couldn't initially resist.

Both Chinese sides eventually united against the invaders but the Japanese responded with amphibious landings and claimed much of Northern China. They then attacked British and US warships that had been dispatched to police the trade routes to the colonies. The US still refused to intervene despite the Japanese bombing one of its gunboats and killing 50 sailors. The League of Nations was impotent in the face of a serious threat to the peace and by 1938 Japanese forces had taken Canton and pushed the Chinese west.

Fascism and communism were already pitted against one another in Spain. The civil war ravaged the country from 1936 while democracy stood powerless between General Francisco Franco's right-wing military and President Manuel Azaña's republic. Hitler saw this as an opportunity to test his forces and he swung the conflict in Franco's favour by contributing aircraft, Panzers and 12,000 men. The Spanish appealed to Britain and France for help but neither was willing to commit resources to fight for democracy. Only Stalin contributed to the republic's war effort because he foresaw the future clash between Nazism and Communism and was keen to keep Hitler occupied away from the Russian border. Thirty thousand volunteers also signed up to fight Fascism in Spain but it wasn't enough and Madrid eventually fell in 1939 with countless civilian deaths.

Italy, too, was flexing its imperialistic muscles in Africa: Mussolini had made his first land-grab by invading Abyssinia (now Ethiopia) in 1935. Emperor Haile Selassie appealed directly to the

Far Left: *Benito Mussolini with the Fascist Blackshirt Youth*

league for help as Italy was part of the union and was threatening a smaller independent state. The league had been established to deal with exactly this kind of dispute but, despite the efforts of Anthony Eden to broker a peace deal, the league was eventually undermined and did nothing.

Mussolini had seized power during a general strike in 1922. He marched on Rome and was asked by the king, Victor Emmanuel, to form a government rather than plunge the country into civil war. He swiftly formed the Fascist Party and banished the remaining parties to the political wilderness. Six years later, the Fascist Grand Council with Mussolini at its head held absolute power in Italy. He also embarked on a massive program of modernising the country's infrastructure, which gave millions of people jobs and made him immensely popular. He then clamped down on the Mafia to minimise corruption before updating the air force and launching several new ships. This allowed them to ride out the Great Depression more easily than most and Mussolini found himself an inspiration to other world leaders.

Hitler saw this fascist ideal as strong and purposeful rather than weak and lethargic, so he modelled his Nazi Party on the Italian system. To the east of Germany, a patchwork of weaker states – Poland, Czechoslovakia, Hungary and Romania – now filled the void. Hitler believed that Germany should expand to give its people more living space but he needed the backing of a revitalised military to ensure swift victory. He'd already broken the terms of the armistice and now he violated the treaty itself by leaving the League of Nations, further developing the Luftwaffe and increasing the size of the navy. He then ordered Hermann Göring to ensure that Germany was ready for war within four years, although he initially believed Britain could be coerced into joining an alliance.

When it became clear that Britain was militarily and economically weak and was adopting an appeasement policy, Hitler branded their leadership 'inadequate' and looked elsewhere, particularly in the Far East. He severed ties with China and formed an alliance with Japan instead. Then he declared that Austria would be incorporated into Germany and made plans to invade Czechoslovakia on the premise that

a good percentage of the population – in the Sudetenland in particular – were German and wanted to return to the Fatherland.

The general reaction was not what Britain expected: the USA remained in splendid isolation with two vast oceans separating it from potential areas of conflict, while the French built the Maginot Line fortifications along their eastern border to wage a purely defensive campaign should war again break out. Britain had no stomach for a fight so they opted for a strategy of diplomacy, negotiation and compromise.

With Hitler now uniting Germany and Austria in a bloodless takeover on the eve of elections that may have

Above: *Neville Chamberlain waves the Munich agreement that he believes will ensure peace throughout Europe*

Above: *Hitler and Mussolini*

leaders were reduced to saying what people wanted to hear and not what they believed. Despite this, Britain did take a hard line: if Germany continued its advance towards Czechoslovakia – a close ally of France – total war might be the only option.

With Austria already having abandoned democracy for National Socialism, the movement now permeated society in Czechoslovakia. The passion and desire to join Germany already existed, however, and it was simply a matter of convincing the people that President Beneš was unable to deliver strong leadership or economic prosperity.

Neville Chamberlain conceded that Britain could not prevent the inevitable if Germany liberated the Sudetenland, even though it would break the Czech agreement with France. So his task at Munich was to convince Beneš to concede ground to Hitler peacefully so that the whole continent wasn't dragged into a war that no one except Hitler wanted or could afford.

But Beneš had already mobilised his army to the border with Germany and was in no mood to concede anything. He believed, mistakenly as it turns out,

thwarted his expansion plans, he continued to look east. A conference was hastily arranged in Munich in October 1938 but it was conducted in front of the world's media and the

that Britain and France would pressure Hitler into backing down. Chamberlain was forced into a corner, and he chose to side with Hitler should the liberation of the Sudetenland proceed. Hitler's main aim, however, was the total conquest of Czechoslovakia, and he now knew that Britain and France would not go to war to protect the country.

On 29th September 1938, Chamberlain asked Beneš to concede the Sudetenland to Germany in the belief that Hitler had no further demands in the region. If he refused, Beneš would be held responsible for any future conflict and his people would receive no help. The Czech president had no option but to sign the agreement. Appeasement, however controversial, appeared to be working.

The democracies in Europe believed that the agreements signed in Munich did away with the oppression and unfairness of Versailles and heralded a new and peaceful era across the continent. Britain conceded that Germany had a moral right to incorporate the Sudetenland into the Reich and believed that Europe was safer than at any time since the last war.

Czechoslovakia was now a divided nation, however, and it fractured along the cracks created by Munich. Hitler was quick to coerce new President Emil Hácha into ceding Bohemia and Moravia to Germany, and he then

Above: *Adolf Hitler as leader of the Axis powers*

dispatched troops to take Prague in strict violation of the Munich agreement.

Britain continued its diplomatic stance, however, and conceded that, as the Czech state was unviable, German intervention did not compromise Munich after all. The mood across Europe was changing rapidly, with public opinion and the media turning against appeasement and calling for Hitler to be opposed.

The more Britain conceded, the more Germany wanted. With Czechoslovakia now under their control, Hitler demanded that the largely German city of Danzig in the Polish Corridor – former German territory that had been given to Poland at the end of World War One – be returned to Germany and that a rail link should be established with East Prussia.

The attitude towards Hitler amongst the Allies had now changed and the cabinet demanded that Chamberlain offer the Poles an alliance. This was the first time that German expansion was vigorously opposed, but the alliance effectively committed Britain to war should Hitler continue pushing east.

Mussolini, meanwhile, sought to emulate Hitler and invaded Albania.

Italian forces easily overcame the Albanian tribal monarchy and Mussolini then set his sights on conquering lands throughout the Balkans and southern Europe so that they could control shipping and trade in the eastern Mediterranean. Britain and France reluctantly accepted Italian aggression and refused to intervene.

Stalin, too, had imperialistic tendencies and he was determined to settle old scores by pushing west towards Germany. These two superpowers had no intention of squaring up to one another so they signed the non-aggression Molotov-Ribbentrop Pact. Foreign Minister Joachim von Ribbentrop assured Hitler that Britain and France would not honour their commitment to Poland so Germany began mobilising troops.

The pact dealt a devastating blow to the Allies because Poland was now at the mercy of the Soviet Union and Germany. And there was no way Britain and France could come to the rescue of the Poles in the face of overwhelming Axis superiority. The Polish leadership knew little of the pact and were confident that if an invasion came Britain and France would intervene in the west and pressure Hitler into splitting his forces.

But the French had no intention of launching an offensive against Germany and were content to sit behind the Maginot Line. Hitler knew this and redeployed most of his troops from the French border east to Poland. The Poles may have been quietly confident but they were outflanked, outnumbered and outgunned, and they didn't have the backing they believed.

Late on 31st August 1939, German SS Troops in Polish uniforms launched a false attack on a German radio station on the border. The following day, Hitler used this and the Polish refusal to cede Danzig as his pretext for invading with two enormous pincer movements from Army Groups North and South. Although he still believed Britain and France would not react, he was mistaken: both countries declared war on Germany on 3rd September, although they weren't able to act immediately as they were unprepared. With no backlash forthcoming, Stalin invaded eastern Poland in mid-September.

Appeasement had given way to abject betrayal and the whole of Europe was plunged into war once more.

Far Left: *Molotov and Ribbentrop sign the non-aggression pact between the Soviet Union and Germany in 1938*

The Evacuation at Dunkirk & the Battle of Britain

Far Right: *The Royal Castle in Warsaw is shelled by the Germans*

By 8th September the inner German pincers had closed around Warsaw, trapping tens of thousands of Polish troops. The outer pincers were circling Brest-Litovsk while the Red Army moved in from the east. Warsaw fought on and refused to surrender until 27th September, however. Under the terms of the Nazi-Soviet Pact, the country was then divided up. Many thousands of Poles who were considered genetically and intellectually inferior were rounded up by the SS and murdered.

With Poland falling to the mechanised German Blitzkrieg in the first few weeks of the war, Hitler turned his attention to the north and west. He initially offered Britain and France a peace settlement because he didn't believe they had the stomach or resources for a prolonged war but he was refused. So, in November 1939, Hitler told his officers that he wanted to attack in the west. His staff were appalled: most of the army was still dealing with Polish stragglers and the campaign hadn't been without its problems, the most serious being that the lightly armoured Panzers were vulnerable and frequently outpaced the following infantry. Hitler reluctantly heeded the advice from his generals and backed down, with the proviso being that they moved the following spring. There followed six months of what the Americans called the 'phoney war'.

success prompted Mussolini, who had maintained Italy's neutrality, to join the war and Allied troops were immediately forced into retreat.

French and British forces had expected to be a match for Germany and they boasted roughly the same number of men, but the German tanks were superior and the Luftwaffe managed to keep the RAF at bay during the first few months of 1940. Britain maintained a large naval advantage but the ships could only impose a blockade on German ports throughout the North Sea and Baltic, and the two navies rarely

In April 1940, Germany invaded Denmark and Norway, both of which succumbed quickly. In May, the German army conquered Luxemburg, the Netherlands and Belgium and advanced into France. Their immediate

encountered each other in combat.

Britain responded with a partial mobilisation, the issuing of gas masks, evacuation of children from the cities and a blackout at night, but these measures were simply not enough to counter the German lightning war. Its blitzkrieg tactics worked as well in the west as they had against Poland and the 100,000 men of the British Expeditionary Force that had been deployed in northern France were about to face a reality check; so too the French army which had advanced several miles into Germany but refused

to push beyond the range of its artillery.

Head of the Kriegsmarine Admiral Karl Dönitz, meanwhile, demanded another 250 submarines so he could cut British supply lines across the North Atlantic. His U-boats had already

Above: *Admiral Karl Dönitz in 1943*

Centre: *German mechanics take a break from repairing a Messerschmitt 109*

Above: *The SS Athenia was the first Allied ship sunk by a U-boat during the war*

misidentified and sunk the liner *SS Athenia* without warning on the first day of the war, which set a dangerous precedent. Twenty-six Americans were among the dead.

The British navy with its 12 battleships and five aircraft carriers dwarfed the German fleet and it immediately declared a total blockade of German ports. This diverted escort ships and other resources away from the Atlantic convoys, however, and the German submarines sunk merchant shipping at will. The aircraft carrier *Courageous* was then sunk by *U-29* and, a few weeks later, *U-47* slipped into Scapa Flow undetected and sank the *Royal Oak*. The Royal Navy gained

partial revenge by tracking down the pocket battleship *Graf Spee* in the South Atlantic but this was a brief blip in what was to descend into total war with all its horrors.

In the spring of 1940 the BEF took up positions along the Belgian border, confident in the knowledge that 100 French divisions were manning the Maginot Line to the south. There was a distinct lack of action, however, so Britain and France sent troops to Finland to help repel Stalin's advancing Red Army. They were unsuccessful and the Russians soon took northern Scandinavia. German forces then overran Norway and Sweden.

When the time finally came to attack

on the Western Front, General Erich von Manstein surprised the Allies by advancing through the Ardennes. The Allies had captured a copy of the original invasion plan, which suggested German troops would attack in the far north of Belgium before sweeping down towards Paris, but von Manstein knew the plans had been captured and were predictable so he moved where the Maginot Line ended. The Allies were prepared for a long defensive campaign and believed their slight numerical superiority would eventually dissuade the German army from advancing. The Nazis held a clear advantage in the air, however, with the Luftwaffe boasting twice as many bombers and a superior fighter in the shape of the Messerschmitt BF109.

On the day Winston Churchill

Above: German soldiers inspect an abandoned Belgian tank

became prime minister, 10th May 1940, Hitler launched his offensive in the west. Army Group B drove straight into Belgium while the Luftwaffe softened up Allied defences. British and French forces in the north, believing the captured invasion plan, advanced to their forward positions without realising that the German Panzers had pushed through the Ardennes and were now

circling behind them to cut them off. Five days later, the Dutch capitulated after the bombing of Rotterdam.

General Heinz Guderian's Panzers then advanced swiftly towards Sedan. French troops were still bogged down in the Maginot Line and could do nothing to help. Three days later the town surrendered. Guderian's Panzers were now 40 miles behind Allied lines

and began pushing north to encircle them. Only now did French supreme commander General Maurice Gamelin realise the danger. He ordered the Allies to retreat, which confused them as they were not under heavy fire at the front. Somewhat surprisingly, French Prime Minister Paul Reynaud then called Churchill and told him that they had been defeated and he intended to surrender.

Guderian disobeyed orders and continued racing west through Amiens and Abbeville to cut off the remaining British troops. The Panzers finally reached the coast at Noyelles but the British prepared to counterattack on 21st May at Arras. The Allied tanks were no match for the Panzers, however, and the following day Guderian moved north once more to finish off the BEF and the French First Army. The latter was soon in full retreat towards Boulogne, Calais and Dunkirk. Further north, Major-General Erwin Rommel had also disobeyed orders and was closing in on Dunkirk.

The British were now trapped in

the port under heavy bombardment with little hope of rescue. General Alan Brooke knew only a miracle could save the BEF – a risky evacuation across the Channel was the only option. Hitler then made a decision that undoubtedly contributed to their escape: the exhausted men of the Panzer divisions had pushed so far beyond their infantry that their lines of supply and communication were stretched to breaking point. Their equipment too was in need of servicing, so they halted their advance when they could have

applied the coup de grâce.

The British made the most of this two-day spell of execution and organised the evacuation as part of Operation Dynamo, which began on 26th May. The following day a motley collection of destroyers, tugs and ferries crossed the Channel to begin rescuing nearly 400,000 men. But most of the ships were too big to approach the beaches and the port was under such heavy bombardment that it couldn't be used. So Vice-Admiral Bertram Ramsay called for all available pleasure craft to assist with the evacuation. Hundreds of civilian cabin cruisers and barges responded and helped ferry the troops from the beaches to the larger ships offshore. The RAF also lent its weight to cause. Despite this, more than 30 Allied ships and a quarter of the little boats were sunk by the Luftwaffe, although the losses would have been much higher had the French rearguard not kept the Panzers at bay for an extra two days.

The French fought on in the south but by the morning of 5th June they were retreating en masse. Four days later the Germans reached the River Seine and on 14th June they marched into Paris and raised the Swastika on the Eiffel Tower. They then turned their attention back to the Maginot Line in the east and quickly overwhelmed the demoralised French resistance.

On 21st June Hitler arrived in Compiègne to sign the armistice in the same railway carriage that had been used to end the First World War in 1918. He handed the French delegation his terms and told them if they didn't agree the Panzers would continue south. They signed the following day. Now only Britain stood in the way of total German domination of Western Europe.

Having overseen the fall of France,

Hitler returned triumphantly to Berlin, where he was greeted by more than a million people. He knew the British situation was hopeless and offered them a generous peace settlement that would allow them to keep their empire as long as he had a free rein in continental Europe. When Churchill stood firm and

Above: *The armistice is signed at Compiägne on behalf of the French by General Charles Huntzinger*

Right: *The last of the few - the only existing Spitfire that fought in the Battle of Britain*

issued his 'fight them on the beaches' speech, Hitler ordered the destruction of the island nation.

Churchill's bravado was admired by the Royal Family and the country at large but no one seemed to be giving any thought as to how Britain might actually win the war. The bulk of their army may have escaped at Dunkirk but their tanks, artillery and other hardware had been lost. They were no match

for German forces now massing on the continent, so it appeared that Britain, like France before it, would have to fight a defensive campaign. Coastal defences were beefed up and the home guard was re-supplied with what weapons and equipment were available.

Hitler now drew up Operation Sea Lion, the invasion of southern England by 20 divisions using converted barges as landing craft. But Grand Admiral Erich

Left: *A squadron of Mark XII Spitfires in 1944*

Raeder was concerned that the British navy was still vastly superior and he would not be able to hold the Channel long enough to land the German army. Hitler knew the Luftwaffe outnumbered the RAF and Hermann Göring assured him that with air supremacy established the landings could still be made.

On 10th July 1940, the Luftwaffe began its campaign against shipping in the Channel. The British countered with their two specialist fighters, the highly manoeuvrable and fast Supermarine Spitfire and the rugged and powerful Hawker Hurricane. The Spitfires targeted the Messerschmitt fighter escorts while the Hurricanes attacked the Dornier, Junkers and Heinkel bombers, but substantial early losses meant the RAF only had 700 aircraft left by mid-July. Outnumbered three-to-one, fighter command

seemed doomed to fail. And if the RAF lost control of the skies above Southern England, Operation Sea Lion would be launched. They had one crucial advantage over the Luftwaffe, however: radar.

Vital information about the number, height, speed and range of enemy aircraft was relayed to Fighter Command HQ at Bentley Priory. When the threat had been assessed in the operations room,

fighters were dispatched to intercept the German aircraft. Göring realised he had to draw more of the RAF into battle so he stepped up the campaign against shipping in the Channel. But Air Chief Marshal Sir Hugh Dowding didn't take the bait and allowed the ships to be targeted without offering air support because he knew he needed planes in reserve for when the real battle for Britain began.

A frustrated Göring upped the ante in mid-August by declaring that he wanted to destroy the RAF in the air and its bases on the ground. The first wave concentrated on the radar towers and airfields on the south coast. Instead of continuing to target the radar towers however, Göring decided they were unimportant, but this was a crucial oversight. The airfields may have taken a superficial hammering but the aircraft were not caught on the ground and none were put out of action for more than a few hours.

German losses were steadily rising while the RAF managed to limit its casualties, but the Luftwaffe was determined to end the contest and launched another wave on 15th August. Some RAF pilots flew seven sorties in one day and they accounted for 92 German aircraft. Dowding tried to

THE CONCISE HISTORY OF **WWII**   37

Right: *Firefighters tackle a blaze during the Luftwaffe's bombing campaign against London*

rotate his exhausted pilots but the RAF was at breaking point. Morale was also plummeting amongst Luftwaffe pilots as their losses continued to mount.

Later in the month a squadron of German bombers lost their bearings and bombed London, so the British responded by attacking Berlin. Targeting the civilian population enraged Hitler and he ordered massive retaliation. With the benefit of hindsight, shifting the point of attack to London was another mistake because it gave the fragile RAF time to regroup and re-arm.

On 15th September, yet another enormous bombing raid was launched against London. But the RAF managed to shoot down enough aircraft to convince Hitler that the skies above Britain could not, for the time being at least, be secured. Sea Lion was postponed indefinitely.

The Battle of Britain had been a decisive engagement, although Hitler's response was to shift the point of attack yet again. With losses during daylight sorties untenable, by mid-October he ordered the bombing raids to target Britain's cities by night: the Blitz had begun. London was attacked almost every night for the next month and the centre of Coventry was levelled. Despite killing 50,000 civilians, Hitler again realised that he couldn't break British spirit so he called off the raids in May 1941 and diverted

German resources east towards former ally Russia.

The Commonwealth and Nazi-occupied countries like Poland and Czechoslovakia had supplied a huge number of pilots for the battle, and it was to them and all the men and women of the RAF that Churchill was speaking when he uttered the immortal lines: "Never in the field of human conflict was so much owed by so many to so few."

Operation Barbarossa and Stalingrad

Far Right: *The plan of attack during Operation Barbarossa*

Although the defeat of Britain and France was seen as a necessity, the conquest of the Soviet Union was Hitler's priority because he felt the Russians posed the greatest threat to a wider German Empire.

Hitler was a passionate anti-communist and believed that if Russia, with its wealth of natural resources and enormous territory, could be subdued, then German expansion east to take advantage of these riches would finally allow his people to become the 'master race'. He also envisaged a time when Germany could not accommodate all of its people and would need to expand simply to feed and house them. Although he'd made these feelings clear in *Mein Kampf* in 1925, Hitler signed the non-aggression Molotov-Ribbentrop Pact with the Soviet Union in 1939. He followed this up with a trade pact in 1940 before he entered the Axis Pact with Japan. This deal made provision for Soviet entry but the two sides were increasingly suspicious of one another and, having been revised by the Russians, it remained unsigned.

Hitler wasn't unduly concerned as it had always been his intention to double-cross Moscow. He stayed at his retreat in the Bavarian Alps in early 1941 and used the time to plan Operation Barbarossa, an all-out assault on the Soviet Union. With France having already fallen to his lightning war, Britain virtually sidelined

after being bombed and starved into submission by the Blitz and the sinking of the Atlantic convoys, and America not yet involved, Hitler could deploy four million men, 600,000 vehicles, 3,000 aircraft and 750,000 horses to the proposed 1,800–mile Eastern Front.

Throughout the summer of 1941 the invasion plans were refined until three separate strikes were agreed: Army Group North would attack through the Baltic States (Lithuania, Latvia and Estonia) and seize Leningrad; Army Group Centre would advance through Poland to Moscow; and Army Group South would march into and take control of the Ukraine and the southern oilfields.

Hitler's generals were surprised by

the plan's ambition and were concerned that three strikes would spread their forces too thinly, but none had the courage of their convictions and voiced their doubts to the Führer. They realised that the Red Army could immediately mobilise three million men and had about the same number in reserve. They also knew that the Russians boasted 20,000 tanks, three times the German force. The Russian tanks were smaller and less powerful so the Nazis were faced with a dilemma: could they overcome a larger but technically inferior opponent before superior numbers eventually wore them down?

Hitler made his move in the early hours of 22nd June 1941 when his artillery opened up on all three fronts. The Luftwaffe struck Soviet airfields at dawn to keep Russian aircraft on the ground and eventually destroyed nearly

4,000 planes for the loss of just 36. The infantry attack was then launched to take advantage of the initial surprise. The tactic seemed to be working and the German Panzers were soon thrusting deep into the Soviet Union.

Two days later, the infantry had already advanced 50 miles. Soviet counterattacks were poorly planned, weak and ineffective, and they were dealt with easily. The Red Army seemed paralysed and unable to defend the borders and thousands of Russian soldiers were captured in the opening skirmishes. A week later, two Panzer divisions surrounded Minsk, trapping 300,000 Red Army troops. In the Ukraine, the Germans were welcomed as liberators because anti-Russian sentiments were rife and the country felt oppressed by Stalin.

Stalin himself was outraged at the

Above: *Soviet POWs are marched west to the concentration camps*

Far Right: *General Georgi Zhukov was largely responsible for halting the German advance into Russia*

Despite having a large part of the Red Army surrounded west of Minsk, General Heinz Guderian of the Second Panzer Group asked Hitler for permission to continue pushing east. He agreed and a week later the tanks had pushed as far as Smolensk, only 250 miles from Moscow.

Army Group South was meeting sterner opposition, however, and they were still more than 50 miles from Kiev. It was then that Hitler ordered Guderian south to help take Kiev. Guderian objected but Hitler overruled him and insisted that Kiev must fall before he turned back towards Moscow. In late August, Guderian headed south against his better judgement.

The Red Army was now fully mobilised with its new T34 tank, which was faster and more manoeuvrable than the Panzer Mark IV. Despite the tougher opposition, the two Panzer groups met east of Kiev in September 1941. Half a million Russians were killed or captured in the engagement, so the tactic seemed to have paid dividends. Hitler was further buoyed with the news from Leningrad: Army Group North had surrounded the city and cut it off. Instead of taking the city by force, however, Hitler decided to lay siege and starve it into submission.

German betrayal, even though he'd seen the offensive coming and had stationed millions of men along the front. On July 3rd he finally addressed the nation, appealing for them to rise up and defend the motherland. It seemed as if the rallying cry had come too late, however. The Panzers were slicing ever deeper into Russia and hope looked lost, but Hitler then made his first tactical blunder of the campaign.

Leningrad was soon brought to its knees, the pitifully small amount of food arriving from the east nowhere near enough to feed the population.

Hitler desperately wanted the offensive over by the winter because he knew the Russians were well-equipped to deal with the conditions and his supply lines would be overextended by then. Winter also meant that the waters around Leningrad froze and food could be brought in over the ice. (Even with supplies increasing, four thousand people a day died from starvation during December.)

Guderian's Panzers had now returned from Kiev to rejoin Army Group Centre in Smolensk before the final assault on Moscow. The Germans enjoyed overwhelming superiority in both men and hardware and they expected to end Soviet resistance by Christmas. Stalin was not prepared to give up without a fight, however. He ordered Marshal Georgi Zhukov to organise the defence of the capital, and the entire civilian population turned out to build fortifications that would hinder the German advance.

The Russian rearguard action was given a boost by the weather, which turned in October. Heavy rain bogged

the ill-equipped German vehicles down in mud and Army Group Centre eventually ground to a halt 50 miles from Moscow. If Hitler hadn't delayed the advance on Moscow when Guderian was in position and the city's defences hadn't been completed, the German Panzers might well have taken Moscow before the winter set in.

Despite being desperately short of food, provisions and arms, the Germans pressed on, and by early December they were just 20 miles from the Kremlin. The bitter cold now took its toll on men and machinery. Tank engines seized, machineguns froze solid and men were incapacitated with frostbite. On 5th December, the advance was halted.

The Russians were given another tonic when Stalin learned from his spies in the Far East that Japan wasn't ready to attack in Siberia. He immediately recalled 30 highly trained and well-equipped divisions – half a million men – to Moscow to bolster the city's defences. As soon as they were in position, they unleashed a ferocious artillery bombardment before battering their way through the German lines in waves of T34s. The savage counterattack lasted a week and dealt a devastating blow to the

German High Command.

Hitler refused to accept responsibility for the tactical blunder and sacked his overall commander of Barbarossa, Field Marshal Walther von Brauchitsch, as well as Heinz Guderian and 35 senior officers.

He then issued a directive stating that German forces should no longer retreat from the Soviet advance and must die fighting instead. German troops initially managed to secure their lines but Stalin then launched a second thrust along the

Right: *General Friedrich Paulus in southern Russia in early 1942*

entire front.

Zhukov was sceptical that a massive counteroffensive would drive the Germans backwards and tried to dissuade him but Stalin wouldn't listen. For the next four months, fierce but ultimately inconclusive battles were fought along the front and Hitler soon realised that a change in strategy would be needed if he was going to defeat the Red Army.

Germany's oil supply was running out so Hitler decided to stop advancing in the north and concentrate on securing Russia's oilfields to the south in the Caucasus. Army Group A would sweep down from Kharkov while Group B covered the northern approach along the River Don to the west of Stalingrad.

The Russians immediately mounted a counter-strike to retake Kharkov, so the Germans retaliated by laying siege to the Crimean port of Sevastapol. The port finally fell to the Nazis in June 1942 so Hitler again pressed for the oilfields, but he then made another series of strategic mistakes that would ultimately cost Germany the war in the east. He ordered Group B to push further east and take Stalingrad even though the city wasn't strategically important. (It was, however, an important industrial centre that produced a quarter of Russia's tanks and other hardware.)

When the Panzers trying to seize the oilfields ran into heavy resistance, Hitler compounded his error by diverting most of the tanks approaching Stalingrad south to help. Bolstered by their arrival, Group A cut off the Soviet armies to the south by linking their forces between the Black Sea and the Caspian. With their oil supply lines severed, Russian forces were on the brink of collapse but Hitler then made another catastrophic error. Believing the Soviets to be outgunned in the south, he sent the bulk of his Panzers back to Stalingrad.

There didn't seem to be a problem initially and Group A advanced on the oilfields. When they arrived, however, they found the wells had been totally destroyed by the retreating Red Army. With their reinforcements having been diverted back to Stalingrad, the German supply lines were overstretched and they could advance no further into the Caucasus.

By late August, German forces had advanced to the outskirts of Stalingrad. The battle for the city would become one of the most crucial engagements of the entire war. The Sixth Army under General Friedrich Paulus crossed the

Don on 17th August 1942 and began a final push into the city in the hope that it would fall before the Russian winter set in again. A week later, their forces had reached the Volga and there was heavy fighting in the suburbs.

Once again, the civilian population was mobilised. (When the Panzers had been diverted to take the oilfields, the people of Stalingrad had used this two-week window to build substantial fortifications.) But the German advance was relentless: Stuka dive bombers preceded the infantry, levelling entire streets before the foot soldiers moved in to search the rubble for stragglers. The fighting was prolonged and particularly brutal as the Russians defended the city house by house and room by room. They used the sewers to communicate and the ruins to snipe, but the Germans continued pushing towards the Volga.

To capture the city named after his sworn enemy was becoming an obsession for Hitler and he instructed General Paulus to make his final push for the river on 4th October. The Panzers rumbled through the streets destroying every building but they were again overextended and the Soviets took advantage of a slowing of the advance to

OPERATION BARBAROSSA AND STALINGRAD

draft in another million troops.

On 19th November they launched a counterattack against a German north flank that was protected by poorly trained and ill-equipped Hungarian and Romanian forces. The Red Army pierced their lines with a division of T34s and a second attack in the south the following day was equally effective, with German infantrymen surrendering in their thousands. Three days later the two pincers met, surrounding the entire German Sixth Army. Paulus could probably have broken out and escaped but Hitler believed the Luftwaffe could supply the army and pressured him into holding his position.

Two weeks later, Marshal Erich von Manstein announced his intention to break through the Soviet lines to relieve the Sixth Army as part of Operation Winter Storm. After two days, Manstein's advance was halted by stiff resistance 30 miles from the city. He promptly instructed Paulus to try breaking out of Stalingrad but Paulus waited for Hitler's permission, which was then refused. It was another critical error.

Zhukov now mounted a massive assault on Manstein's Panzers and drove them back, leaving the Sixth Army effectively abandoned. They needed nearly 1,000 tons of supplies every day to survive but the Luftwaffe couldn' air drop more than a tenth of that. The Russian air force took advantage of the indecision and weak supply lines and soon controlled the skies.

In the dead of another bitter winter the Red Army advanced on the 200,000 men trapped in the city. On 8th January 1943 they asked the German

to surrender but Paulus refused. By the end of the month, however, he had no option but to concede defeat. Of the 100,000 men who surrendered, only 5,000 would return to Germany after the war.

German supply lines were broken, their troops demoralised, and the Russians, who could call on huge reserves of men and machinery, were now able to rout their forces along the entire front. Zhukov pushed into the Caucasus to confront Army Group A. If he made it to Rostov, the large part of the German army that had pushed beyond the Black Sea to the Caspian would be cut off. Hitler was left with no choice but to order Group A to withdraw and fight an aggressive guerrilla-style rearguard action.

In late January, Zhukov ordered another massive offensive along a 500–

mile front from south of Rostov to Kursk in the north. Despite fighting a brilliant tactical retreat, von Manstein's forces were outnumbered seven to one and the Red Army destroyed huge numbers of tanks and guns as well as killing another million German infantrymen.

The Russians were now being re-supplied by Britain and America so they were able to continue their push west, but Hitler wasn't convinced they had the firepower and planned a major counter-offensive with a new batch of Tiger and Panther tanks at Kursk in the summer. Zhukov's spies warned him of the offensive, however, so he supervised the installation of anti-tank defences, minefields and miles of barbed wire. He also drafted in huge numbers of men and machinery from less important areas along the front. On the eve of the assault, his forces vastly outnumbered the Germans.

The Red Army's artillery bombardment should have dissuaded the Panzers from advancing but they rolled towards Kursk anyway. The offensive was a complete disaster. Fifty thousand German soldiers and 500 tanks were lost.

THE CONCISE HISTORY OF **WWII**

Above: A captured German POW

Despite these heavy losses, the Panzers still pushed into the city, but Zhukov was waiting with another 900 tanks.

The largest armoured battle of the war saw the Soviet T34s pierce the German lines and strike at point-blank range. The retreating Germans lost another 400 tanks in a single day. Overhead, the Soviet Air Force finally established its superiority over the Luftwaffe and the combined forces drove Germany back. The Battle of Kursk was the last major German offensive on the Eastern Front.

Barbarossa and Stalingrad highlighted the enormous human cost of the conflict. The battle for the city resulted in the deaths of approximately one million men and the loss of countless tanks, aircraft and artillery pieces on both sides. Overall, Barbarossa cost more than five million lives in 1941 alone. It was the largest and bloodiest single military campaign in history, and there's no doubt that poor planning and execution on the part of the German High Command contributed to their heaviest defeat. The operation is also cited as the major turning point of the war in the east.

From Pearl Harbor to Midway

America may have been supplying Britain in the continuing conflict in Europe via the Atlantic convoys but the country was not officially at war. That changed on the morning of 7th December 1941 when forces of the Empire of Japan launched an unprovoked surprise attack on the American Pacific fleet at anchor in Pearl Harbor. By the end of the day, more than 20 warships had been hit, 188 aircraft had been destroyed and 2,400 men had been killed.

The following day, President Franklin Roosevelt declared war on Japan.

The Japanese reasoned that America was about to enter the war alongside Britain and decided to try knocking the mighty adversary out before it was actually on a war footing. A lightning strike at Pearl Harbor was designed to cripple the US fleet and discourage the country from entering the war in the first place. In reality, the attack woke a sleeping giant and eventually contributed to the destruction of the Japanese Empire in 1945.

In August 1940, Japan took advantage of the French defeat in Europe and seized control of French airbases in northern Indochina. The Japanese demanded to be given access to airbases and other strategic positions throughout the territory but the French refused. Japan promptly invaded the entire colony to further their imperial pretensions in the Far East. America immediately froze

Japan's overseas assets and limited their ability to buy oil. The choice for Japan became clear: back down and lose face or continue to seize territory in the region to warn the US. The aggressive General Hideki Tōjō immediately ordered Japanese forces to attack all territories held by France, Britain, the Netherlands and the United States.

Japan was expecting to overrun Allied positions and occupy their territories within months. They also believed that the US didn't have the stomach for a lengthy war with thousands of casualties and thought they'd capitulate if the strikes showed their overwhelming superiority, both in terms of military hardware and tactics. If they could destroy the US fleet, they reasoned the US would sue for peace in the Pacific theatre.

As commander of the Imperial Japanese fleet, Admiral Isoroku Yamamoto was given the task of drawing up plans for an attack on Pearl Harbor. He had two battleships, nine destroyers, countless smaller ships, 30 submarines and six aircraft carriers at his disposal. The carriers could deploy hundreds of the latest Mitsubishi Zero fighters which were faster, more manoeuvrable and carried heavier weapons than their American counterparts.

The US fleet, on the other hand, comprised eight battleships that were relics of the First World War, eight cruisers, 30 destroyers and two carriers.

Yamamoto was confident of victory over an inferior force but he still planned the attack with great care. His spies had infiltrated the local population several months before the attack and the Americans were far more concerned about sabotage from an enemy already on the islands.

However, as the months passed and no sabotage was reported on the ships, and no enemy aircraft were reported in the skies above Pearl, the threat began to fade and the Americans became complacent. Gun batteries were left unmanned on Sundays and crews were given extended leave. They were even more confident that there couldn't be a torpedo attack in the harbour because the waters were too shallow for conventional torpedoes to stabilise, but a worrying precedent had been set a year earlier and US forces should have been on high alert.

Yamamoto had studied the only

other similar engagement: the British aerial torpedo assault on the Italian port of Taranto on the night of 11th November 1940. One battleship was sunk and another two ships were severely damaged. Two months later, the Japanese conducted tests with torpedo bombers against obsolete ships in the East China Sea, but, because of the shallow water in Pearl Harbor, they began working on weapons with wooden box fins on their tails that were similar to those used by the British.

To ensure that the Americans had no idea they were about to strike, the Japanese navy gathered in Tankan Bay in the North Pacific in complete radio silence. On 26th November 1941, the fleet left its anchorage and sailed for Hawaii. To complete the façade, Japanese delegates arrived in Washington to broker a deal that would see their forces withdraw from China, a country they'd been at war with since 1937.

Above: *One of the Japanese Ko-hyoteki-class midget submarines*

Early on the morning of 7th December the Japanese fleet moved into position north of Hawaii. Just after midnight, five Japanese midget submarines separated from their mother subs and spread out around the narrow mouth of the harbour. One was sunk at sunrise by the outdated American destroyer *USS Ward*, which meant that the attack actually began at sea and that the Americans fired first.

On the bridge of the *Ward*, Captain William Outerbridge sent a coded warning up the chain of command but it wasn't acted upon and the main air attack later that morning wasn't anticipated. A second opportunity to intercept the incoming fighters was missed when army privates Joe Lockard and George Elliot, who were manning the Opana radar station on the north coast of Oahu, picked up a large contact approaching from the northwest. Just after seven in the morning, they

Above: *An American aircraft hangar is destroyed by fighter-bombers*

called the switchboard operator at the administration and information centre to let Lieutenant Kermit Tyler know about the inbound aircraft. Tyler assumed it was a scheduled flight of American B-17s from the US mainland and told Lockard not to worry.

As the first wave of 183 fighters and bombers dived in from the west, American forces were stirring on another fine Hawaiian morning. The slower and more vulnerable torpedo bombers attacked battleship row just before eight o'clock, while the faster dive bombers attacked the airfields inland. The second wave of 170 aircraft then bombed the crippled fleet.

A second midget submarine now made it through the line of torpedo nets into the harbour itself. It fired on the *USS Curtis* but missed. The American destroyer *USS Monaghan* retaliated by ramming and sinking the submarine. A third sub was found washed up

Above: *Mitsubishi Zeroes on the flight deck of the carrier Shokaku prepare to launch the second wave of attacks*

on the beach in eastern Oahu the following morning after its gyro compass malfunctioned. The fourth of five was found in a neighbouring lagoon in 1960. A good deal of mystery sounded the last midget submarine but photos taken from Japanese reconnaissance aircraft during the attack appear to show it inside the harbour firing on the *USS West Virginia*.

Surprise had won the day for the Japanese because the overconfident American military leaders on the island, Admiral Husband Kimmel and General Walter Short, didn't believe such an attack was possible. Despite a good deal of confusion amongst the Japanese pilots – flares that told the dive bombers and torpedo bombers in which order to attack were misinterpreted and the entire air force attacked at once – tactically, the strike was a masterstroke, but, with hindsight, it was a strategic disaster because it finally called the US to action.

The two American aircraft carriers, which were a primary target, were not in Pearl at the time and Admiral Nagumo failed to launch a third wave to find and destroy them along with the fuel depots, repair facilities, the submarine base and the intelligence station. Had he launched another wave instead of being satisfied with what they'd achieved and turning for home, the attack might have finished the US in the Pacific.

American losses were considerable: the *Arizona*'s forward magazine exploded, killing more than 1,000 men and sinking the ship; the *Oklahoma*, *West Virginia* and *California* were sunk with the loss of 600 lives (the latter two would return to service, however); and fourteen more ships were damaged, some seriously.

Lieutenant Tyler may have become one of the villains of the piece, but there was no early-warning system in place on Hawaii. No flight crews were on duty at any of the islands' airfields so none of the American aircraft could have been scrambled in time to intercept the

Above: *President Franklin Roosevelt signs the declaration of war against Japan on 8th December 1941*

Japanese fighters. The few P36s and P40s that made it into the air during the battle itself were outnumbered and outclassed by the new Mitsubishi Zeroes. Even if the infrastructure had been in place to scramble the pilots from when the radar contact was made, most of the American aircraft were not flight ready and needed re-arming and refuelling. In fact they

were lined up wingtip to wingtip at Wheeler Field and Hickam Field. As soon as one had been attacked and was on fire, the destruction simply spread along the line.

The Americans immediately launched a salvage operation. By mid-1942, five battleships and two cruisers had been refloated. The *Arizona* and *Utah* were too badly damaged, however, and remain as war memorials.

President Roosevelt was incandescent with rage and delivered his famous 'Infamy' speech to congress the day after the attack. He then declared that a state of war existed between the two countries. At the same time, the Japanese were landing in the northeast of Malaya. They easily overcame the British-Indian troops defending the territory. A second incursion into Thailand was virtually unopposed and 30,000 Japanese were soon marching down the east coast of Malaya towards Singapore, the centre for British rule in the area.

All of the British guns defending the city were pointing south in anticipation of attack from the sea, however. The only option was to send the new battleship *Prince of Wales* and the battle cruiser *Repulse* back up the coast to

intercept Japanese troop transports. Japanese bombers attacked and sunk the ships within two hours with the loss of 1,000 men. It was now clear that the era of the battleship was over. Aircraft launched from carriers easily penetrated their defences and could sink them with bombs or torpedoes, which had happened at Pearl Harbor and again in Malaya.

The British withdrew to Singapore where they hoped their force of around 100,000 would be enough to see off the Japanese. Even without their heavy artillery, they should have been able to hold out but Japanese air strikes reduced their defences to rubble and they pushed

Above: *The American B-25s line up on the USS Hornet's deck before the Dolittle Raid*

through the flimsy British lines in only four days. General Arthur Percival surrendered with 90,000 men. It was a humiliating defeat for a man who had his enemy outnumbered three to one.

In the Philippines, the United States also capitulated. Japanese bombers wiped out their aerial advantage by destroying their aircraft on the ground at Clark Field. When their ground troops landed, the Philippine army folded and Manila fell within ten days. US forces withdrew to the Bataan Peninsula to wait for relief but reinforcements didn't arrive in time. In April 1942, the Japanese launched a major offensive and broke through the American lines. They were left with no option but to surrender, leaving only the British colony of Burma standing against the land of the rising sun.

Japan attacked in the south against outdated British defences and only 15,000 men. They rallied with a brief counterattack but the Japanese quickly crushed the uprising and within two months had taken Rangoon.

In only six months, Japan had taken the western Pacific Rim, inflicting crushing defeats on the US at Pearl Harbor and in the Philippines, and over the British in Malaya and Burma.

In retaliation for Pearl Harbor, the Americans launched a bombing campaign – known as the Doolittle Raid after Lieutenant Jimmy Doolittle – against Tokyo in April 1942. Sixteen B-25 Mitchells launched from the deck of the *USS Hornet* 700 miles from Tokyo. They were too big to land on the carrier after their mission so they would have to be flown into China. Simultaneous raids struck Yokohoma, Kobe and Nagoya in an effort to raise morale after endless Japanese victories.

Although little material damage was done by the bombing, and only about 50 Japanese civilians were killed, the psychological impact was far greater. The Japanese now knew they could be reached by American forces in their homeland. This led to Admiral Yamamoto recommending that Japan extend its sphere of influence in the Pacific so that no US forces could reach Tokyo.

As Japan already controlled most of the coastline to the west in China, Southeast Asia, the Dutch East Indies and the Philippines, they decided to push south into Papua New Guinea and the Solomon Islands. They also had to take the island of Midway in the Pacific because it was from there that US forces were refuelling.

In May 1942, the operation to broaden their defensive position was launched. The Solomon Islands fell first, and, two days later, the Japanese carriers entered the Coral Sea to begin their attack on Papua New Guinea. Admiral Chester Nimitz had predicted the attack, however, and he ordered two carriers

and a number of smaller ships into the area. The fleets circled one another for two days before American aircraft sank the carrier *Shōhō*. The Japanese retaliated by sinking a destroyer and then hitting the carrier *Yorktown*. The carrier *Lexington* was also struck by bombs and torpedoes and was eventually scuttled. The Americans responded by attacking the carrier *Shōkaku* but the first wave of torpedo bombers couldn't break through the Japanese Zeroes. A second wave eventually crippled the carrier, however. After two days, the sides disengaged to lick their wounds.

In terms of ships lost, the Japanese could claim victory but the Americans viewed it as a major strategic and tactical success as they'd prevented the Japanese advance into Papua New Guinea, the first time the empire had been repelled since Pearl Harbor. With the sides deadlocked in the South Pacific, Japan took the rash and ultimately catastrophic decision to try taking Midway with another lightning strike.

Victory would have strengthened their position in the theatre considerably: defeat was unthinkable as it would leave mainland Japan vulnerable to attack by American bombers.

Far Right: *USS Yorktown is struck by a torpedo during the Battle of Midway*

The Battle of Midway

With Japanese and American forces arm-wrestling for superiority in the Coral Sea, Japan was already drawing up plans to invade the vital strategic island of Midway. American code-breakers intercepted Japanese transmissions identifying Target AF as their next objective but they couldn't be sure where this attack would happen.

Midway was one possibility as it offered an ideal point from which to launch another attack on the US fleet in Pearl Harbor. One of the airbases on Midway was instructed to send an open communication detailing problems with the island's water system in the hope that the Japanese would intercept it and then pass it on to the task group. The plan worked perfectly: the Japanese informed its fleet that Target AF was having water-supply issues.

Nimitz now knew the enemy was approaching, but he believed their attack was too complicated. Japan initially intended to launch a diversionary strike north into the Aleutian Islands to draw part of the US fleet away from Hawaii. This would leave Midway lightly defended and, when the weakened American fleet responded to the invasion, they would be ambushed by four carriers, two mighty battleships and a fleet of smaller ships.

Pre-warned to the Japanese plan, Nimitz ordered his carriers to surprise the Japanese fleet before it was in position. On 4th June 1942, Japan launched its small attack on the Aleutian Islands. Nimitz refused to split his forces, and he also allowed the subsequent air attack on Midway to proceed unopposed, except for sending up a few outdated Brewster Buffaloes that were easily shot down by the superior Zeroes. Despite this rather token resistance, the air assault on the island was blunted.

Admiral Chūichi Nagumo had kept some of his aircraft loaded with torpedoes in case the US fleet was spotted but he now ordered the planes reloaded with fragmentation and incendiary bombs for another attack on the island. No sooner had the ordnance been swapped than part of the American fleet was spotted on the horizon. Nagumo was caught in two minds and eventually decided to launch a second strike on Midway rather than attack the US fleet.

Before many of the bombers had

even taken off, aircraft from the American carriers began bombing the Japanese ships. Nagumo scrambled all of his Zeroes to bring them down and they repelled the first attack but he now knew that the fleet contained American carriers and they were the priority target. He gambled again and had the Japanese aircraft re-armed with torpedoes and bombs for use against the US carriers.

The delay would cost him dearly, although the gamble initially seemed to have paid off when the first wave of outdated American torpedo bombers were shot down by his defences. With his own aircraft finally ready to launch, high-altitude American dive bombers slipped through undetected and dropped their ordnance on the Japanese fleet. The entire complexion of the battle changed in five devastating minutes when three of the Japanese carriers were mortally wounded.

The carrier *Hiryū* had managed to avoid being hit and now launched a small counter-strike, its aircraft seriously damaging the *USS Yorktown*. The American carrier didn't sink immediately but it was later torpedoed by the *I-168* and eventually sank on 7th June. Aircraft from the *Enterprise* retaliated against the *Hiryū* that afternoon with the loss of four hundred lives.

The engagement had been a tactical disaster for the Japanese, the damage sustained by its fleet irreparable. Indeed historians have since called the battle the most decisive victory in the history of naval warfare. With the Japanese navy unable to keep pace with its losses, and with the US fleet being bolstered by men and machinery, it was only a matter of time before the gains made by the Japanese Empire in the Pacific were reclaimed by America and her Allies. The Battle of Midway marked the beginning of the end for Japan.

The North Africa Campaign and the Italian Surrender

By 1940 British forces had been ejected from northern France but, instead of trying to take back the ground conceded to Germany, Churchill diverted his remaining resources to North Africa and only returned to France with the Americans on D-Day in 1944. During these four years, Stalin's Russia bore the brunt of the conflict with the Nazis on the terrible Eastern Front.

Having been brought into the war by the Japanese in late 1941, Roosevelt firmly believed that the fight in Europe should be targeted directly at Germany across the English Channel, but the Americans were newcomers to the war and Churchill convinced them to attack easier targets in North Africa and the Mediterranean, what he called Hitler's soft underbelly.

This underbelly wasn't as soft as Churchill believed, however, and it wasn't long before Allied troops were bogged down in a war of attrition against a determined enemy. The Red Army, on the other hand, was at last making progress on the Eastern Front and was heading for the real prize: Berlin. So why did Churchill concentrate on the Mediterranean instead of helping the Russians by splitting German forces?

There's no doubt that the preservation of empire and a fear of a return to trench warfare in the north of France played a role in his decision, but there was more to it than that. Churchill may have

appeared resolute in the face of adversity during the retreat from Dunkirk and the Battle of Britain but he was a leader under pressure who was acutely aware that Britain, if the Atlantic blockade by German U-boats continued unchecked, would probably lose the war. The reality was that the conflict was exposing Churchill's soft underbelly.

When he received news that 33,000 men at Tobruk, a vital port in Libya, had surrendered after a daring German move to cut the city's supply lines in June 1942, he was mortified. The neglected defences had been weak and the far smaller German army had taken advantage of low morale to force the British to capitulate. Churchill saw it as a disgrace but, more than that, it opened the way for Field Marshal Erwin

Above: *Erwin Rommel discusses his options in the North African desert*

Rommel to attack vital strategic targets like the Suez Canal in Egypt. Coming just after the fall of Singapore, when 90,000 Allied soldiers had surrendered to a vastly inferior Japanese force, it was another blow to British morale. More defeats in Norway, Greece and Crete heaped humiliation upon humiliation.

Conventional thinking at the beginning of the war was that Britain was still a global power because of its vast empire, but these disasters were weakening the country and were damaging for its leader. Churchill had fought on the frontiers in India, Sudan and South Africa and knew that

protecting the empire was almost as important as defending the islands during the Battle of Britain.

When Italy joined the conflict on Germany's side in June 1940, Churchill felt even more threatened in the Mediterranean. Mussolini could call upon a powerful navy, and Italy already had colonies in Africa, so, if he could brush the British aside in Libya and Egypt before taking Cairo, that would be the coup de grâce for the British Empire.

Churchill had to counter the Italian threat and desperately needed morale-boosting victories so he ordered half his tanks to Egypt, his priority being

to preserve the empire's supply lines through the Suez Canal. These supply lines guaranteed oil from the Persian Gulf and troops from India and Australasia, without which the British war effort would falter.

Mussolini's optimism was misplaced and he overestimated his army's ability to fight a desert campaign. The British counterattacked during Operation Compass under Major-General Richard O'Connor, driving deep into Libya and routing the retreating Italians. It seemed that Churchill's gamble would pay off.

Hitler was so concerned about taking the canal that he sent Rommel, the Desert Fox, to Libya with divisions of tanks and elite troops in February 1941. Rommel was an unconventional but tactically astute leader who often ignored instructions from the High Command and repeatedly outmanoeuvred the British. His Afrika Korps would attack unexpectedly and gradually pushed a British Eighth Army – weakened after sending reinforcements to Greece – back towards Cairo. Despite several counterattacks by both sides, by early 1942 Britain had ceded Benghazi and Gazala and much of western Egypt, and their position in North Africa was once again on a knife-edge.

Churchill had been concentrating on beefing up the air force and navy, and this led to under-funding and chronic shortages within the army, which was now the weakest it had been since the Great War. The prime minister had to save face so he launched a massive recruitment drive. Soldiers needed to be trained in the art of desert warfare so they could take on Rommel, but they were young and inexperienced, and so were their commanders. Chief of the Imperial General Staff Sir Alan Brooke even went as far as saying that half of the entire military wing was unfit for purpose. He blamed the inadequacies on the First World War, which had robbed this generation of their most talented officers. To cap it all, Churchill's leadership was now being questioned and he had to

fend off two votes of no confidence in the Commons.

As if this wasn't bad enough, the colonies now began to question British rule. Future Chancellor Stafford Cripps had already drawn up plans to give India independence, and Egypt was also clamouring for the end of imperial rule from London. Rommel, in fact, was looked upon as a liberator.

The British reacted with heavy hands: Ambassador Sir Miles Lampson marched into King Farouk's palace and demanded that he form a pro-British Egyptian government or abdicate. Farouk chose the former, although Egypt officially remained neutral until the last year of the war, by which time the fighting had long-since ceased.

It seemed that only a decisive British

Right:
*Montgomery
supervises the
Allied advance in
November 1942*

Far Right:
*General George
Marshall was an
astute tactician*

victory in the desert could save the empire. Instead, the humiliation at Tobruk seemed to have sealed its fate and Churchill began to unravel. His only hope now lay with nurturing a special relationship with the Americans.

His first priority, however, was to fly to Africa and sack the commanders who had allowed Rommel to within striking distance of Cairo. He replaced them with General Bernard Montgomery, a man determined to toughen up the troops and take no more backward steps. Montgomery's confidence and informality endeared him to the rack and file, and by October 1942 the army was ready to attack Rommel's inferior force at Alamein.

Montgomery was also fortified with news from Britain's decoders at Bletchley

Park. They had broken the German Enigma Code and knew where and when to find German convoys re-supplying Rommel, as well as his tank movements in the desert. On 23rd October 1942, Montgomery launched his artillery bombardment. Instead of securing quick victory with an overwhelming number of tanks, however, the British were forced to pick their way through enormous minefields, and the battle soon turned into an infantry arm-wrestle which hung in the balance for nearly two weeks. In the final reckoning, it was Rommel who conceded defeat and ended up in full retreat. This was the British army's first victory over the Germans, and it guaranteed Churchill's position for the rest of the war.

He called it the decisive land battle of the conflict, but this was merely rhetoric to boost morale. The reality was that the British had lost more men in the engagement and Montgomery's cautious pursuit allowed Rommel and the majority of his Afrika Korps to escape. The Americans were not impressed with either the motive for the campaign or the outcome. They believed it was a selfish attempt by the British to cling on to colonial power when the real fight lay

against Hitler in Europe.

As early as April 1942 General George Marshall visited Britain to outline his plans for a second front in France. The British were unconvinced by his timetable – he wanted to launch the attack by Christmas – but praised Marshall's boldness and promised to go along with the plan, with one important reservation: they had to be allowed to continue their defence of India and the Middle East. Churchill was clearly still the senior partner in the alliance but power was shifting perceptibly to the Americans. The prime minister was also concerned that the US would only be able to contribute a couple of divisions to the new front if they moved in 1942, so the majority of the troops would have to come from the Commonwealth, notably Canada.

A lightning raid on the Channel port of Dieppe in late 1942 showed just how fragile the Allies were. The Canadians lost seventy percent of their men during the disastrous assault. It proved to be a costly but ultimately worthwhile lesson because it dissuaded the Americans from going ahead with an all-out attack, a campaign they would surely have lost.

Churchill instead convinced the Americans and Russians that France was Hitler's tough snout, whereas a second front in Italy would continue striking at his soft underbelly. The thinking was that the British army would have more luck against the weaker Italian military, and defeating Mussolini would ensure the security of the British Empire.

Marshall wasn't convinced but he wasn't prepared to overrule Churchill by going behind his back to Roosevelt. The president was facing hostility at home from a people who wanted peace with Hitler so they could concentrate on avenging Pearl Harbor. He desperately needed American blood to be shed in direct conflict with the Nazis so that the country would unite against the Axis Powers. Roosevelt therefore gave the green light to Operation Torch, an invasion of North Africa that would trap the retreating Rommel.

Churchill let him select the commander for the operation, so Roosevelt chose Dwight Eisenhower because he had a better relationship with the British officers. It was the biggest amphibious assault to date, dwarfing the Gallipoli landings during the First World War. The initial advances were positive

Above: *General George Patton shares a joke with Admiral Hewitt on the USS Augusta off North Africa in 1942*

and the Allies confidently predicted that they'd oust Rommel from the continent by Christmas.

Hitler had other ideas, however. He rushed troops and supplies into Tunisia so Rommel could make a last stand. In one engagement at the Kasserine Pass, the new American recruits were routed and driven back 85 miles in a week. Churchill and Brooke were now more determined than ever to end the campaign in North Africa before striking at Italy, but Marshall didn't believe the war could be won here. Churchill overruled him and was finally vindicated

with the capture of Tunis in early 1943. They took a dozen German generals and 250,000 men prisoner, but the victory came six months after Stalingrad and the Axis soon recovered.

Marshall again lobbied for the second front in France, but Churchill knew they still didn't have the men or resources to mount the offensive so the Americans beach-hopped across the Mediterranean instead. The landings at Sicily proved just how fragile their alliance was, however. They lost 20,000 men in the first month and the relationship between Montgomery and his American counterparts, George Patton in particular,

almost reached breaking point.

They managed to stay civil until Sicily fell, by which time Mussolini's Fascists were about to be overthrown. The new leadership surrendered and tried to join the Allies but, instead of being able to draw on their support, Montgomery and Patton were pitched against German forces in the north.

With the Americans still pushing for the second front, Churchill decided to shore up Italian defences, secure the Balkans, take the islands in the Aegean, intensify the bombing campaign against Germany and, lastly, build up American troops in Britain in preparation for

the future invasion of France. In other words, the second front was still bottom of his list of priorities.

The code-breakers at Bletchley Park had intelligence that once the Allies had a firm hold in Italy, the Germans would retreat north. This would give the Allies room to strike at the industrial centres in southern Germany. But Hitler again surprised them by standing firm in Rome and drawing them into a war of attrition. They also fought a guerrilla-style campaign in the mountains and kept the Allies at bay for the winter of 1943-44.

Churchill had expected an easy time

in the Aegean but the German defence was again resolute. Brooke believed the prime minister was spreading his forces too thinly around the islands when Italy needed to be finished off. Marshall and Roosevelt backed him up and informed Churchill that Operation Overlord would take place with or without his consent in the spring of 1944.

Churchill, Roosevelt and Stalin met in Tehran in 1943 in tense circumstances. Stalin's Red Army was pushing the Germans back through the Ukraine and the Americans were finally making progress in the Far East. Churchill was under pressure as never

Above: The German-held monastery at Monte Cassino lies in ruins after some of the bloodiest fighting of the war

Right: The Polish war cemetery at Monte Cassino

before. Roosevelt and Stalin insisted that the Allies struck in France, so Churchill was again outvoted. With Russia and America fully mobilised, he was increasingly marginalised as the junior partner and this filled him with resentment. On the return journey to London he suffered two minor heart attacks.

During his recovery, he decided to launch a final offensive in Italy to convince Stalin and Roosevelt that Britain was still a force. The landings at Anzio were successful but the troops failed to press home their advantage and were soon pinned down by German bombers. The sides slugged it out in particularly brutal engagements such as at the German-held monastery of Monte Cassino.

Despite taking severe casualties, the Allied bombers eventually levelled the monastery, but the Germans fought on for five months in the rubble. It was akin to the Somme in its brutality but the Germans eventually capitulated. General Mark Clark's Fifth Army then broke out from the beachhead and liberated Rome, but his moment in the spotlight was overshadowed when the Allies launched Overlord in Normandy the following day.

D-Day and the Soviet Advance in the East

Far Right:
General Eisenhower rallies the 101st Airborne in the build-up to D-Day

Churchill had long been opposed to landing men on the beaches of Normandy but he was eventually talked into agreeing Operation Neptune (the landings themselves) as part of the broader Operation Overlord. The Americans had been pushing for a second front against the Nazis in France but Churchill was so concerned about the strength of his army that he convinced Roosevelt to attack German and Italian forces in North Africa and the Mediterranean instead. By 1944, however, he could no longer keep the Americans out of Europe.

There were several dummy raids planned along the coast in the Pas-de-Calais, and such was the success of the disinformation spread in the spring that Hitler refused to beef up his defences further west. Heavy bombers then dropped aluminium strips over the Straits of Dover to convince German radar operators that there was a large invasion force gathering offshore. Bad weather forced the Allies to delay the assault by a day but on 6th June 1944 they were ready.

Under the leadership of General Dwight Eisenhower the invasion fleet, comprising more than 1,000 warships, 4,000 transport ships and landing craft, and another 1,500 ancillary craft and merchant vessels, boasted 195,000 naval personnel, of whom nearly two thirds were British, one third were

Above: *American troops come ashore on Omaha Beach*

American and the minority came from the remaining Allies. It was and remains the largest combined operation in military history.

Having broken the German codes and spread disinformation about the attack happening near Calais, the fleet bombarded weaker German positions on five beaches, codenamed Omaha, Utah, Gold, Juno and Sword. The Atlantic Wall built by German forces occupying Northern France may have been weaker in Normandy but the fighting once the bombardment had stopped and the landing craft had moved onto the beaches was both brutal and bloody. The struggle to secure Omaha Beach was particularly fierce.

Rommel had been recalled from North Africa and had spent a year preparing for the invasion, but the Germans were confident in their existing defences having seen off the raid at Dieppe in 1942. The French Resistance helped provide the Allies with vital information on the beaches and the pillboxes and bunkers guarding them, and the beaches themselves were carefully chosen for their topography. The Germans could still call on more than a million men and countless Panzers and artillery guns. Rommel was concerned that the Allies might not strike where he anticipated, so he bolstered the defences along nearly 2,000 miles of coastline.

The defenders wrongly believed that the weather was still too bad for amphibious landings and many divisions were stood down. Rommel was even given time off to celebrate his wife's birthday. The British Sixth Airborne Division took advantage of this tactical error and were dropped with Canadian troops by glider behind enemy lines as part of Operation Deadstick. Each glider carried 30 men or a jeep, or a six-pound field gun.

Their objectives were to capture the bridges across the Caen Canal and the River Orne, to destroy the German

Above: *British troops looking for cover on Sword Beach*

Merville artillery battery and to destroy the bridges over the River Dives. The German 716th Infantry Division and 21st Panzer Division counterattacked at dawn but, despite taking heavy casualties, the airborne troops held out until they were relieved by special service commandos. By 12th June they'd achieved all their goals.

The American 82nd and 101st

Above: *Canadian soldiers are about to be surprised on Juno Beach*

Airborne weren't as fortunate: 13,000 troops jumped at night but they were widely dispersed over the landing area and found it difficult to rendezvous. The Germans were similarly confused and couldn't mount an effective counter-strike.

At three o'clock in the morning, the aerial bombardment began at Sword Beach. A little later, the navy opened up to soften the remaining German defences. By seven-thirty British infantrymen were pouring ashore with little resistance but as they fought their way inland the fighting became much tougher. They wouldn't achieve their

THE CONCISE HISTORY OF **WWII**

main objective – capturing Caen – for another month despite joining up with the Sixth Airborne by the end of the first day.

The Canadian forces at Juno Beach faced much sterner opposition in the form of two heavy and nine medium batteries along with countless machinegun nests and pillboxes. Despite coming ashore with heavy armour themselves, they lost half the men from the first wave. However, 30,000 troops of the Third Infantry eventually fought their way over the German seawall and advanced inland against the 21st and 12th Panzer Divisions of the Hitler Youth.

Twenty-five thousand men of the British Second Army under Lieutenant-General Miles Dempsey landed at Gold Beach. The German defences were strong and they suffered heavy casualties, but the Northumbrian Infantry eventually broke through and made it to the outskirts of Bayeux. Without the help of the struggling Sherman tanks, the last commando unit advanced towards the small port of Bessin.

Omaha Beach was the most heavily fortified and it pitted the First and 29th Infantry of the US Army against the German 352nd Infantry in the Bayeux Zone and the 716th in the Caen Zone. The aerial and naval bombardment had been largely ineffective and there were artillery, mortar and machinegun positions along the bluffs. Most of the tanks failed to make it ashore and ten percent of the 50,000 troops were killed in the first few hours. The beachhead wasn't secure and the D-Day objectives weren't finally achieved until three days later.

The landings at Utah Beach were far more successful and only 200 lives were lost. By the end of the day, 20,000 men of the Fourth Infantry had linked up with the parachute regiments of the 101st Airborne and they advanced swiftly inland against light German resistance.

By the middle of June, most of the units were firmly established inland and they then began the long, slow push east into Germany. On the Eastern Front the Red Army had also been enjoying notable successes. Earlier in the year they'd finally liberated Leningrad after the longest siege in military history. They then took the Crimea and Ukraine, although they couldn't overcome Army Group North in Estonia. On 22nd June, however, they launched a huge offensive in Belarus that resulted in the almost complete

Right: *American troops find a German slumped over the remains of his Panzer*

destruction of Army Group Centre. They then advanced into Romania and Bulgaria where local troops joined the fight against the Nazis. Yugoslavia, Greece and Albania followed, although Hungary only fell with the liberation of Budapest in February 1945, but by then German forces in the east were in full retreat.

In the west, Paris was liberated by Allied and French Resistance troops on 25th August, but a major airborne assault into the Netherlands was unsuccessful so they continued pushing into Germany from the south. German tanks launched a massive counterattack in the Ardennes Forest in December 1944 but their objectives – capturing Antwerp and splitting the Allied lines – were not achieved and they pulled back in January. In February the Allies entered Germany and pushed east towards the Rhine while the Red Army drove through Poland, Silesia and Pomerania. The noose was tightening around Hitler's neck as the war entered its endgame.

The advancing Red Army could never have known what they would find as they entered Poland and eastern Germany, however.

The Final Solution

In the latter part of the 19th century, a school of thought began to emerge in Germany and Austro-Hungary that Jewish people were trying to infiltrate elite society and challenge Aryan supremacy. This movement soon had a name – Völkisch – and it called the Jews predators who should be stripped of their citizenship and, if necessary, exterminated for the good of the German people.

Heinrich Class, leader of one faction, wrote in his 1912 best-seller that Jews – which was defined as anyone having a single Jewish grandparent or being a member of the religion on the day the German Empire came into existence in 1871 – should be forbidden from owning land, working in journalism or banking, or holding public office. This institutionalised anti-Semitism was dealt a blow when the Völkisch parties were defeated in the 1912 elections but, instead of consigning the policy to history, it was then incorporated by the mainstream parties.

The National Socialist German Workers' Party, which would become the Nazi Party, was a direct descendant of the Völkisch movement and they adopted the biological discrimination and fierce anti-Semitism of their predecessors. There was even talk of mass euthanization of the mentally ill and incurable during the economic downturn in the 1920s so more money could be freed up to help the biologically

Above: *Heinrich Himmler inspects Dachau Concentration Camp in 1936*

fit. This radical idea soon spread to the ethnic cleansing of the Jews.

Hitler had already outlined his plans for ridding the continent of the Jewish people in *Mein Kampf* but he initially planned to drive them from Germany rather than exterminating them. In private, however, his views were more extreme and he even suggested building rows of gallows in all the major town squares to hang every Jew in Germany. He wasn't able to put his master-plan into

action until he'd assumed power and by then the Reich had divided its enemies into three distinct groups: the work-shy, habitual criminals and homosexuals were moral opponents and classed as wayward national comrades; as were the political opponents like Marxists, liberals and reactionaries; but the Jews were viewed as racial enemies who had to be removed from society.

When Hitler came to power in 1933 after a campaign of barely disguised violence and oppression, he immediately set up the first concentration camp at Dachau. The following year, more camps were set up outside the cities and run by the Schutzstaffel (SS). They were initially filled with social democrats and

the 'mentally and physically depraved', but Hitler wanted to include Jews so he gradually restricted their social, legal and economic rights. In April, Hitler called for a week-long boycott of Jewish businesses – his first openly anti-Semitic campaign – but it collapsed after a day due to a lack of support. Instead he passed laws excluding Jews from holding public or service positions. It was followed by laws to prevent inferior people reproducing and involved mass sterilizations.

Two years later, he went even further by introducing the Blood Law which stripped Jews of their citizenship and all civil rights and forbade them from interacting with Aryans. Hitler then claimed that if the Jewish question could not be solved by these laws then the problem would be handed over to the Nazis for a final solution. (The term 'final solution' had been used since about 1931, although it did not hint at the horrors to come.)

Throughout the 1930s Jews left Germany in huge numbers. When Albert Einstein returned home after a visit to the US in 1933 he found he'd been expelled from the Kaiser Wilhelm Society and the Prussian Academy of Sciences and he never set foot in

Above: *Joseph Goebbels decorates members of the Hitler Youth*

Germany again. He believed Hitler had induced a psychic illness of the masses, or what we might call mass hypnotism, and there's no doubt that the Führer's extraordinary oratorical skills won over his many doubters.

As if there wasn't enough tension between the Nazis and Jews already, on 7th November 1938, Herschel Grünspan assassinated German diplomat Ernst vom Rath in Paris. The Nazis claimed this had enraged the German public and used it as a pretext to launch vicious attacks on Jewish businesses and synagogues, which culminated in Kristallnacht, the night of broken glass. Thirty thousand were transported to the concentration camps, but most were eventually released providing they handed over their assets to the Nazis and promised to leave the country.

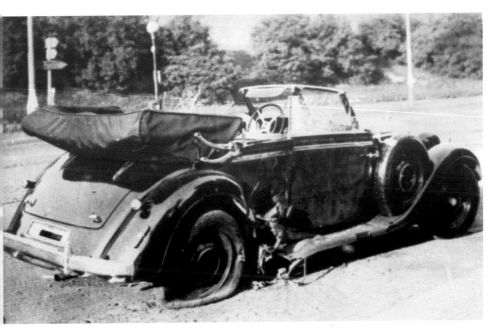

Above:
*Heydrich's
Mercedes after
the assassination
attempt in Prague
that eventually led
to his death*

Hitler then began a program of repatriation but he refused to allow Jews expelled from Germany to settle in former German colonies like Southwest Africa and instead asked Britain and France to accept them in Rhodesia and Madagascar. Reinhard Heydrich, who was director of the Reich's security office, called this mass deportation a 'territorial final solution' and Adolf Eichmann enthusiastically carried out the plan until it was rendered obsolete when the mass extermination of Jews began in 1941.

On the sixth anniversary of his accession to power in January 1939, and only eight months from the beginning of the war, Hitler brazenly predicted the end for the Jews: "If Jewish financiers succeed in plunging us into a war then the result will be the annihilation of the

Right: *Babi Yar ravine in Kiev*

Right: *Babi Yar ravine in Kiev*

Jews in Europe."

With lightning victory over Poland a formality, the question then arose as to what should be done with the two million Polish Jews. Heydrich wanted them put to work in ghettos on the main railway lines to support the war effort. When they had been virtually worked to death, they would be deported, by which of course he meant exterminated. Thousands died of malnutrition, disease and exhaustion before they could be deported so there was still no official program for systematically eradicating the Jews. This enforced labour was just as effective, but some within the Nazi Party saw it as a waste of human resources. Indeed, had the Jews been looked after during their incarceration, they may well have contributed much more to the war effort, especially as Germany was about to invade the Soviet Union and needed all the hardware it could muster.

Three years later, in December 1941, Hitler again addressed the party, prompting Joseph Goebbels to write that the destruction of the Jews was a necessary consequence of the war. The world was too preoccupied with the conflict to notice that they were now being exterminated in huge numbers.

The concentration camps were originally designed to corral slave labourers and Nazi objectors and it wasn't until 1942 that eight became dedicated killing centres. (It should be stressed that although the mortality rates were extremely high in camps like Dachau and Belsen, they were solely for enemies of the Nazi regime and were not used as extermination centres like Auschwitz and Treblinka.) Indeed,

POWs and Jews were usually worked to death, with those who survived their initial incarceration shot or gassed when they were no longer capable of working. For those who were confined to the ghettos rather than the camps, life was equally appalling: 400,000 people were crammed into the Warsaw ghetto, with 40,000 dying from disease and starvation in 1941 alone.

The German invasion of the Soviet Union saw the Holocaust intensify dramatically. There were around three million Jews living in the occupied territories of Poland, Estonia, Latvia, Lithuania, Belarus and the Ukraine to the west of the Eastern Front, and the locals were encouraged to purge Jews from their communities. This was overseen by Einsatzgruppen (SS task groups) that slaughtered Jews by the tens of thousand in western Russia, most notoriously at the Babi Yar ravine outside Kiev in September 1941.

There was then a shift in policy by the death squads. Instead of shooting people they developed mobile gas vans. Three of these units killed 90,000 in a single month, and the gas chamber was soon adopted as an alternative in the camps. Between 22nd July and

12th September 1942, 300,000 people were deported from Warsaw to the Treblinka extermination camp. The plan outlined at the Wannsee Conference earlier in the year had been to round up the seven million Jews in the Soviet Union, Hungary and the other occupied territories and transport them by train to camps like Auschwitz, and this operation was now in full swing.

It is a sad truth that in the early years of their persecution by the Nazis, Britain, the US and their remaining Allies did little to help Jews escape from Germany and some actively opposed their deportation. There is also little doubt that Britain and the United States knew about the death camps by 1942 – indeed radio broadcasts to that effect were transmitted throughout Europe – but they were too preoccupied with fighting the Axis in the Mediterranean and in the Far East to do anything about them. A bombing campaign was clearly not a viable option either as it would have killed thousands in collateral damage.

It is equally tragic that most of the prisoners had no idea what fate awaited them in the camps. On arrival they would be instructed to strip before entering the 'showers' for delousing. They were told that hot meals and drinks were waiting for them so they entered of their own will. They were then gassed with hydrogen cyanide – up to 2,000 at a time – before having all their jewellery and gold fillings removed. The bodies were initially dumped in pits and covered with lime but most were dug up later and burned.

There was the occasional uprising against the Nazis, notably in the Warsaw ghetto in January 1943 when thousands of poorly armed Jews held the SS at bay for a month. When they were finally overcome, 13,000 had been killed and a further 60,000 were then deported and gassed. A number of smaller episodes were quickly crushed by the camp guards, although many Jews did escape and fight with the Soviets against their oppressors. For the vast majority, however, the only way to avoid the gas chamber was to bargain with or bribe German officers, although precious few actually survived the war.

By 1943 Germany was on the back foot and hundreds of thousands of displaced people were being taken by rail to the death camps. By the spring of 1944, 8,000 people a day were

being gassed at Auschwitz. At his trial, Commandant of the Camp Rudolf Höss (not to be confused with Hess) claimed to have gassed 400,000 Hungarian Jews in three months.

News of these atrocities had by now spread across the continent, mostly by way of the pitifully few escapees, although the only man to volunteer to be incarcerated, Polish Army Captain Witold Pilecki, wasn't initially believed when he delivered his reports of mass killings at Auschwitz. International outrage at these revelations led to

Right: *Glasses were removed from every new arrival at the death camps*

the halting of mass deportations from Hungary to Auschwitz, but the truth of the matter is that nearly 90% of the Jewish population in Germany and Eastern Europe had already been exterminated. Throughout the continent, 70% is an oft-cited figure.

As the Soviet Union pushed west into Poland, the Nazis dismantled the death camps, dynamited the gas chambers and crematoria and instructed Polish farmers to plant crops where the camps had stood. They then forced the last remaining inmates to march west to the camps deeper inside Germany. Another quarter of a million Jews died on these death marches.

The camps were finally liberated by the Red Army, the Americans and the British in late 1944 and throughout 1945. Despite the retreating Germans attempting to cover their tracks, what the Allies found appalled them: there were 13,000 corpses awaiting burial at Belsen, for example.

The overall death toll in the camps is incalculable, but the best estimates suggest six million Jews and a further five million Soviet POWs, ethnic Poles, disabled people, homosexuals and religious enemies were exterminated.

The Fall of Berlin

Having taken Budapest and repelled several German counterattacks, the Red Army marched into Austria in March 1945. The Wehrmacht had lost more than a million men and countless artillery weapons and tanks defending the Eastern Front the previous year and they were no longer in a position to defend the Reich. Vienna fell on 13th April so the Russians then pushed into Germany itself.

Hitler appointed master defensive technician General Gotthard Heinrici as Commander-in-Chief of Army Group Vistula and tasked him with defending the capital. Heinrici flooded the Oder River by releasing water from a reservoir and built three armour belts, including anti-tank ditches and bunkers, around Berlin.

The Russians had been bolstered by the arrival of the Second Belorussian Front and they now moved into the Seelow Heights, the last major defensive line around Berlin. After four days of heavy fighting in mid-April, and with the loss of 12,000 men, the German lines were breached. Stalin now ordered one prong to join up with American forces on the banks of the Elbe in the south while two more surrounded the remains of the German Ninth Army and thrust into Berlin.

On 20th April, the First Belorussian Front began bombarding Berlin and they didn't stop until they'd fired more

ordnance into the city than that dropped by British and American bombers in the previous five years. By 25th April, Berlin was completely surrounded but, to avoid friendly fire casualties, the Allies held their positions and allowed Soviet forces to enter the city.

By now Hitler knew the war was lost. He'd already berated his generals for their incompetence and treachery and vowed to shoot himself before the Russians could take him. Despite his acceptance of defeat, however, he knew he could still call upon 40,000 regular troops and about the same number of police, boys in the Hitler Youth and World War One veterans.

Stalin, on the other hand, had more than a million men under his command and they advanced into the city centre along the Frankfurter Allee, Sonnen Allee and Potsdamer Platz, and from the north towards the Reichstag. The heaviest fighting was centred around the Moltke Bridge, Alexanderplatz and Havel Bridge but the Red Army soon had a foothold in the city centre.

With Soviet forces closing in on the Reichstag, General Helmuth Weilding realised his only chance of escape lay in abandoning their positions and trying to slip through the Russian lines. Only Hitler could approve the plan but he refused to surrender at a subsequent meeting. Outside, the Russian tanks gave way to General Zhukov's infantry for the final assault on the parliament building 200 metres from Hitler's bunker. Despite meeting fierce resistance from the SS on the upper levels, they fought their way inside and eventually captured the Reichstag on the morning of 30th April 1945.

The Führer then summoned his private adjutant, Otto Günsche, to his chamber. Hitler explained that his staff had failed him and the Red Army would soon overrun their positions. He instructed Günsche to get a can of petrol so that his body could be burned instead of exhibited after his death. He then lined his staff up to thank them before giving Weilding permission to try to escape and then returning to his private quarters. Günsche waited outside for fifteen minutes before Martin Bormann entered to confirm that Hitler and Eva Braun had killed themselves. The bodies were removed by his valet, Heinz Linge, and taken via an emergency exit to the garden of the Reich Chancellery where they were repeatedly doused with petrol and burned. The remains, along with those of Hitler's two dogs, the entire Goebbels family and General Hans Krebs, were discovered by the Red Army in a shell crater and removed shortly afterwards.

(The remains were apparently repeatedly buried and exhumed before being loaded in wooden boxes and shipped to Magdeburg. These were then cremated in 1970 and the ashes scattered in the Biederitz River, although a fragment of the jawbone and part of the skull with a bullet hole were preserved. Recent DNA tests have cast doubt on their authenticity, however, with the skull appearing to be that of a woman in her thirties.)

Hitler's remaining generals immediately begged for peace and the war in Europe was declared over on 7th May. The treaty was signed in Berlin the following day, although the remains of Germany's Army Group Centre held out in Prague until the 11th.

Under the terms of the agreement, Austria was declared a neutral state, while Germany was divided up into zones of administration under British, American, Polish, French and Russian control. As before, however, the boundaries agreed by the Allies were difficult to police and there were feelings of resentment and anger across the continent. There were also deep suspicions in the West about Stalin's motives and goals, and Europe

was soon divided again. In the east, the Warsaw Pact saw Poland, East Germany, the Baltic States, Czechoslovakia, Romania and Albania become Soviet satellites with unpopular communist regimes. West Germany and West Berlin came under the protection of NATO, however, which only heightened the tension in central Europe and led to the Cold War.

Peace in the Far East

By 1945, the war in the Pacific was in its fourth year. The conflict had turned into a brutal and bloody arm-wrestle for outposts like the Mariana Islands, Iwo Jima, Midway, Okinawa and the Philippines. With most of the outlying islands secure by June 1945, preparations were well underway for the invasion of Japan under the codename Operation Downfall.

This invasion was planned in two parts. The first, Operation Olympic, would begin in October and involved landing the US Sixth Army with the intention of taking the southern end of the island of Kyūshū. In March 1946, Operation Coronet would see the First, Eighth and 10th Armies take the Kantō plain near Tokyo on the island of Honshū.

The Japanese had plenty of time to prepare for the invasion and could mobilise more than two million frontline troops and four million reservists, plus there was also a civilian militia of 28 million. With the US having taken Okinawa, both sides learned from the engagement and predicted enormous casualties on both sides if the US were to invade the mainland. Up to 20 million Japanese civilians and military personnel, and at least a million Allied soldiers, would die during the endgame.

These figures were so high that the Allies were forced to rethink their strategy for ending the war. They began

a massive firebombing campaign that destroyed several cities, but that only seemed to make the Japanese more resilient and they began stockpiling munitions to repel the invasion. (On the night of 9th March 1945, an estimated 100,000 Japanese were killed during the firebombing of Tokyo.) The Allies even contemplated using poison gas but opted instead to drop leaflets urging the Japanese to surrender lest they be completely annihilated.

Above: *Colonel Paul Tibbets (centre) named his B-29 Enola Gay after his mother but immediately regretted doing so*

THE CONCISE HISTORY OF **WWII**

With Japan refusing to admit defeat and accept unconditional surrender, however, President Truman was forced to contemplate invading. But he was also facing pressure from the public to end the war and bring their troops home so he asked Prime Minister Clement Attlee if he was right to use the weapon they'd jointly been developing that could end the war immediately. Attlee agreed that the atomic bomb should be used as a military and political weapon, the latter to dissuade Stalin from making further advances in the Far East.

On 5th August 1945, Truman issued an order to the 509th Composite Group on Tinian Island in the Marianas. Their mission was to drop *Little Boy*, a uranium bomb, on Hiroshima the following day. Colonel Paul Tibbets had been training for the run with modified B-29s for three months but his crew still wasn't prepared for the news that the new bomb would carry the power of around 15,000 tons of TNT. (The largest conventional bomb dropped in the war was the Barnes Wallis-designed five-ton Tallboy, which only carried two tons of explosive.)

Early on the morning of 6th August, the B-29, christened *Enola Gay* after Tibbets's mother, took off from Tinian and headed north towards Japan. She was accompanied by observation and instrumentation aircraft that would document the results. By half past seven, the bomb was armed so Tibbets began climbing to 30,000 feet. He then received confirmation from a meteorological aircraft ahead of them that Hiroshima, their primary target, a city that had swollen to around 300,000 people after the fire bombing of other towns, was visible beneath scattered cloud.

The first aircraft was spotted from the ground and an air-raid alert was sounded across the city, but it was lifted when radar confirmed there were only a few planes, which the Japanese believed to be reconnaissance aircraft.

In the belly of the *Enola Gay*, bombardier Thomas Ferebee spotted the T-shaped Aioi Bridge spanning the Ota River and dropped the bomb at 9.15am. Forty-three seconds later it detonated at around 2,000 feet above the city centre. An estimated 80,000 people were killed instantly in the 15-million-degree fireball, including 20,000 military personnel. About the same number were injured, mostly blinded by the light or burnt by the horrific heat, although both numbers would rise significantly due to radiation poisoning. More than two thirds of the population would eventually succumb to the bomb, and around 70% of the city's buildings were destroyed.

The *Enola Gay* was struck by several shockwaves but she had already swung round and was heading for Okinawa. When the aircraft finally made it back to Tinian, the crew was decorated and enjoyed a welcome-home party.

Later that day, General Leslie Groves, director of the Manhattan project that produced the bomb, contacted physicist Doctor Robert Oppenheimer to congratulate him on his creation. But Oppenheimer, having heard about the enormous destruction, was unsure about the ethical implications of deploying such a weapon and many of his team were concerned that it could lead to retaliatory strikes in the future.

President Truman learned of the outcome while returning to the United States from the Potsdam Conference on the *USS Augusta*. He was said to be pleased with the results and sent yet another ultimatum to the Japanese: surrender or face more of the same. The

Japanese saw things differently, however, because with all communications down and the city largely destroyed, they could not appreciate the scale of the disaster. Accurate reports did not reach

Emperor Hirohito for at least 36 hours and he still refused to surrender. In fact he then asked Stalin for help.

On 8th August, Japanese Foreign Minister Shigenori Tōgō was authorised to contact the Russians and ask them to mediate a proposed peace deal between Japan and the Allies. But Stalin refused: he was concerned that the balance of power had shifted to the west and he

knew that the Americans would not hesitate to use another nuclear weapon. He responded by declaring war on the Japanese in the hope that he could further his imperial pretensions in the Far East.

The following morning the Russians launched Operation August Storm against the Japanese along the Manchurian border with over a million troops, 5,000 tanks and 26,000 field guns. The weary Japanese were overwhelmed and Soviet forces moved into North Korea.

President Truman was immediately concerned that Stalin would try to occupy strategic territory in Korea, Japan and throughout the Far East. He'd already claimed much of Eastern Europe and suspicions were running high. Truman knew he had to act quickly if he was going to stop Stalin claiming more territory in the region but he was faced with a dilemma: welcome the Soviet Union into the war and see them overrun the mainland, or temper that welcome with a warning to stay clear of American interests. He chose the latter to show Stalin he meant business and had the technological know-how to win any future conflict,

so he authorised the use of a second atomic bomb: *Fat Man*.

The mission was brought forward two days and the device was loaded onto a second B-29 nicknamed *Bockscar*. Major Charles Sweeney swapped aircraft with Captain Frederick Bock at the last moment and took command for the flight to Kokura, home to a massive military arsenal on the northern tip of Kyūshū. In the event of poor weather over the target, the secondary objective would be the industrial town of Nagasaki.

Bockscar took off from Tinian in the early hours of 9th August in the middle of a tropical storm. It was then discovered that the aircraft had a faulty fuel pump so Sweeney had to climb above the storm to conserve fuel. By mid-morning they were above Kokura but cloud and smog obscured the target, so, after three runs across the city, which used up valuable fuel, they aborted and headed for Nagasaki.

Sweeney knew that if Nagasaki was also obscured by cloud he was in real trouble because they didn't have enough fuel to carry a five-ton bomb to the nearest friendly airbase on Okinawa. When the aircraft arrived at Nagasaki,

Far Left: *The crew of Bockscar*

the city was also covered with cloud so the crew decided to go for a radar-guided drop, but a brief gap opened up at just after eleven in the morning. Bombardier Captain Kermit Beahan dropped the plutonium implosion device halfway between the Mitsubishi Steel & Arms Works in the south and the Ordnance Works in the north.

At 22 kilotons, the yield was considerably higher than *Little Boy* but part of the city was protected by hills. Despite this, the 4,000-degree heat and 1,000km/h winds killed up to 60,000 people instantly, with at least another 20,000 succumbing to injuries and

Right: *Hermann Göring (left) in the dock at Nuremburg for his war crimes*

THE CONCISE HISTORY OF **WWII**

radiation poisoning by the end of the year.

If the Japanese chose to fight on by adhering to the principles of total war, one city after another would be erased so Emperor Hirohito was left with no option but to urge the supreme war council to admit defeat and surrender. The Imperial High Command couldn't agree on the terms, however, so the Allies resumed their conventional bombing campaign against strategic military targets. On 12th August, Hirohito informed the imperial family of his decision to accept the terms of the Potsdam Treaty and surrendered, providing he remained on the throne.

But US Secretary of State James Burns refused to accept this condition and said that everyone in Japan would be treated equally by General Douglas MacArthur. Burns even suggested trying the emperor as a war criminal and sentencing him to death if he was found guilty. MacArthur appreciated how important the role of the emperor was to the Japanese people and was outraged at such a suggestion. It was one thing to defeat an enemy in battle but to humiliate them afterwards was unacceptable.

The Allied terms were amended so that the Japanese throne would be

PEACE IN THE FAR EAST

Far Right:
Emperor Hirohito finally convinced the Japanese war council to admit defeat

preserved and Hirohito delivered his capitulation announcement on 15th August. There was extra pressure to sign the agreement because the Soviet Union was now within striking distance of Japan and communism and the emperor system were totally incompatible. The only way to ensure their traditional way of life therefore was to reach the agreement solely with the Americans. There was a brief rebellion by loyal troops opposed to the surrender but it soon petered out. Two weeks later the agreement was formally signed aboard the *USS Missouri*.

There was initial delight at the way the atomic bombs had ended the war so quickly, but reports from Japan – especially those containing photographs of the damage and human casualties from ground zero in both cities – were heavily censored. When the full horror of the atomic holocaust finally became known there was an upsurge in hostility towards using weapons of this kind again.

The bombs may have brought about the end of the war but at what cost? It's difficult to assess accurately but on Okinawa and Iwo Jima more than 95% of the Japanese defenders were killed because they refused to surrender. If the same happened on the main islands of Japan, casualty figures would have run into the millions, certainly more than the 250,000 killed by the bombings.

Others argue that by stepping up the firebombing campaign, and with Stalin having torn up his alliance with Japan and advancing through Korea, it was only a matter of time before Hirohito surrendered anyway. It seemed an invasion of Japan *was* now a viable option because with Stalin onside troop casualties would be minimised. Truman even noted in his diary that from 15th August onwards, the Soviet Union would have entered the war against Japan. This now became Truman's deadline because he was desperate to end the war without Stalin's help lest the latter continue his aggressive seizure of land in Eastern Europe and the Far East. The Soviet Union had been ravaged by war and the loss of 20 million men but it was recovering fast and was growing powerful, too powerful for Truman's liking.

We will never know if dropping the bombs was ethically or morally correct, or if lives were saved in the long-term, but we do know that they contributed to ending the bloodiest war in history.

Although casualty figures are unreliable because deaths were not recorded accurately, it is estimated that 60 million people died during the war, most from genocide, disease and starvation rather than in battle. The Soviet Union bore the brunt of the horrors and lost nearly 30 million, while eight million Chinese died during the Japanese occupation.

Although the economies of the US, West Germany, France and Japan recovered quickly, Britain remained mired in depression for nearly two decades and the overall cost of the war is impossible to calculate.

The German High Command were rounded up and sent to trial for war crimes at the Palace of Justice in Nuremburg. The first of these tried 23 political and military leaders of the Third Reich, although Hitler, Himmler and Goebbels had all committed suicide by then and Martin Bormann was almost certainly dead. Those found guilty were sentenced to death by hanging.

None of the Allies were tried for war crimes despite various accusations of brutality against the occupying forces in Germany.

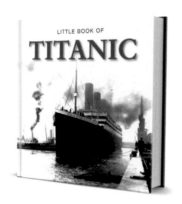

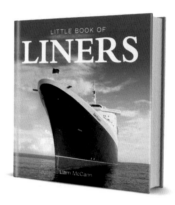

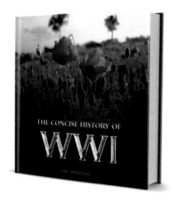

ALSO AVAILABLE IN THE LITTLE BOOK SERIES

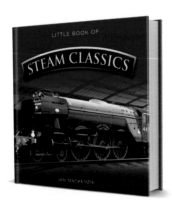

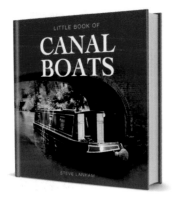

The pictures in this book were provided courtesy of the following:

WIKIMEDIA COMMONS

Design & Artwork: SCOTT GIARNESE

Published by: DEMAND MEDIA LIMITED & G2 ENTERTAINMENT LIMITED

Publishers: JASON FENWICK & JULES GAMMOND

Written by: LIAM McCANN